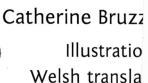

START
W[ELSH]

Catherine Bruzz[one]

Illustratio[ns]

Welsh transla[tion]

Cynnw[ys]

Special note for learners!

The key Welsh phrases you will learn are numbered on each spread. There are also extra words you will need for the activities. By the end of the book you will have learnt 50 Welsh phrases and lots of useful Welsh words. There is a summary of all these at the back of the book.

Pronouncing Welsh

The simple pronunciation guide will help but it cannot be completely accurate. Read the words as naturally as possible as if they were English. Put the stress on the letters underlined e.g. pedoowar. Ask for help from someone who speaks Welsh and try to speak without the guide as soon as you can.

Helô!

Have some fun saying hello and goodbye in Welsh. You need to match the right greeting to the pictures, according to the time of day illustrated. Say the correct phrase out loud. You can check your answers on page 32.

1

Helô, bore da
hello, boh-rah-<u>dah</u>
Hello, good morning

2

Hwyl fawr
hooeel vahoor
Goodbye

3

Noswaith dda
noss-waheth <u>thah</u>
Good evening

4

Nos da
noss <u>dah</u>
Goodnight

Words to Know

Helô!
hello!
Hello!

Hwyl fawr
hooeel vahooor
Goodbye

Wela i di'n fuan
<u>*wel-ah-ee deen vee-ahn*</u>
See you soon

dydd
deeth
day

noswaith
noss-waheth
evening

nos
noss
night

3

Fy enw i yw . . .

Ask your friends or family to play this naming game with you. One person needs to be blindfolded and twirled round. They then have to 'find' someone and ask **Beth yw dy enw di?** The person answers **Fy enw i yw . . .** and says **A ti?** Take it in turns to be the 'finder'. You could all choose a Welsh name!

5

Beth yw dy enw di?
beth ewe duh <u>enn</u>-oow dee
What's your name?

6

Fy enw i yw . . .
vuh <u>enn</u>-oow ee ewe
My name is . . .

10

Pen-blwydd hapus!
pen-bl-oow-eeth <u>*hap*</u>-*iss*
Happy birthday!

Look at the numbers on the inside front cover if you want to ask some older people their ages!

Numbers! Rhifau!

1	**un**	*een*
2	**dau**	*dahee*
3	**tri**	*tree*
4	**pedwar**	<u>*ped*</u>*oowar*
5	**pump**	*pimp*
6	**chwech**	*choo-ehch*
7	**saith**	*saheeth*

8	**wyth**	*oiy-th*
9	**naw**	*nahoow*
10	**deg**	*dehg*
11	**un deg un / un ar ddeg**	
	een dehg <u>een</u> / een ahr-<u>theg</u>	
12	**un deg dau / deuddeg**	
	een dehg <u>dahee</u> / <u>day</u>-theg	

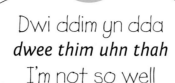

13

Dwi ddim yn dda
dwee thim uhn thah
I'm not so well

Words to Know

Ofnadwy
oh-v <u>nahd</u>-oo
Awful

Gwych
goo-eech
Excellent

Eithaf da
ay-th av dah
Quite well

Da iawn
dah yawhn
Very good

Gweddol
goow-eh-thol
So-so

Diolch
deeohlch
Thank you / Thanks

Words to Know

If you see a * next to a word, it means that it is feminine.

llyfr
lluh-vir
book

pensil lliw
pen-sill llioo
colour pencil

pen
pen
pen

pensil
pen-sill
pencil

glud
gleed
glue

rhwbiwr
rhoob-ee-oowr
rubber

papur
pap-ihr
paper

*riwl
rule
ruler

11

aderyn
ah-dehr-in
bird

*****pêl**
pehl
ball

18

...yw e / hi
... eew eh / hee
... uhd ee oh / hee
It's a...

rycsac
rucksack
backpack

*****mainc**
mine-ck
bench

bachgen
bahch-gehn
boy

Remember, in Welsh, every thing is either
male or female / masculine or feminine.
For masculine we say 'e' and for feminine we
say 'hi'. The feminine words are marked with a *.

13

Words to Know

Dyma'r . . .
dum-ahr
Here's the . . .

*ferch
vehr-ch
daughter

mab
mahb
son

*fam
vam
mother

rhieni
rhee-<u>any</u>
parents

baban
<u>ba</u>-ban
baby

tad
tahd
father

*chwaer
chooaeer
the sister

*fam-gu
vam-<u>ghee</u>
grandmother

brawd
braood
brother

tad-cu
tahd-<u>kee</u>
grandfather

cathod
kath-odd
cats

(yr) haul
uhr haheel
(the) sun

coed
coyd
trees

hwyaid
hoowee-ah-eed
ducks

moch
mohch
pigs

corynnod
cor-run-odd
spiders

cŵn
coown
dogs

17

27

Dwi'n byw yn y dre
dween beyoow uhn uh dray
I live in (the) town

28

Dwi'n byw yn y wlad
dween beyoow uhn uh w-lad
I live in the country

The Shopping List / Rhestr siopa
r-hess-tr shop-ah

afalau
ah-val-eye
apples

mefus
mehv-ees
strawberries

bananas
bananas
bananas

grawnwin
grahoon-ooeen
grapes

moron
mohr-ohn
carrots

tatws
tah-toos
potatoes

tomatos
tomatoes
tomatoes

letys
lettuce
lettuce

Gwydraid o ddŵr
goow-eed-ride o thoor
A glass of water

Menu / Bwydlen bw-eed-len

sudd oren
seethe ohr-ehn
an orange juice

gwydraid o ddŵr
goow-eed-ride o th-oow-r
a glass of water

gwydraid o laeth /lefrith
goow-eed-ride o lah-eith / leh-vreeth
a glass of milk

darn o gacen
darne o gack-en
a piece of cake

iogwrt
yog-oort
yogurt

ffrwyth
froowth
fruit

bara
bah-ra
bread

caws
cow-s
cheese

creision
craysh-eon
crisps

Beth wyt ti eisiau wneud?

You need two or more people to play this acting game.
Read the phrases and then cover them up. One of you
asks **Beth wyt ti eisiau wneud?** and acts out one of
the activities. The other player, or players, answer
Dwi eisiau . . . whatever they think the activity is.
Take it in turns to be the actor.

36

Beth wyt ti eisiau wneud?
behth oiy-t tee eh-shy neighd
What do you want to do?

37

Dwi eisiau gwylio'r teledu
dwee eh-shy gweel-ee-ohr tel-e-dee
I want to watch TV

38

. . . chwarae pêl-droed
. . . *chwah-r-eye pehl-droheed*
. . . to play football

39

. . . seiclo
. . . *say-klo*
. . . to cycle

40

. . . mynd i nofio
. . . *mihnd ee noh-vee-oh*
. . . to go swimming

Words to Know

Wyt ti eisiau . . .?
oiy-t tee eh-shy
Do you want to . . .?

Ydw
uhd-oo
Yes, I'd like to

Nac ydw, dim diolch
nack uhd-oo, dihm deeohlch
No thanks

Pa liw yw e?

Here's a fun game to help you practise colours in Welsh with your friends or family. You will need a dice and some counters. When you land on a square all the other players shout **Pa liw yw e?** (**Pa liw ydy o?** is used in north Wales). You say **Fy hoff liw i yw coch** or whatever colour you have landed on. If you get the answer wrong you miss a turn. Good luck!

41

Pa liw yw e?
parr lioow ewe eh
What colour is it?

START

42

Beth yw dy hoff liw di?
behth ewe duh hoff lioow dee
What's your favourite colour?

FINISH

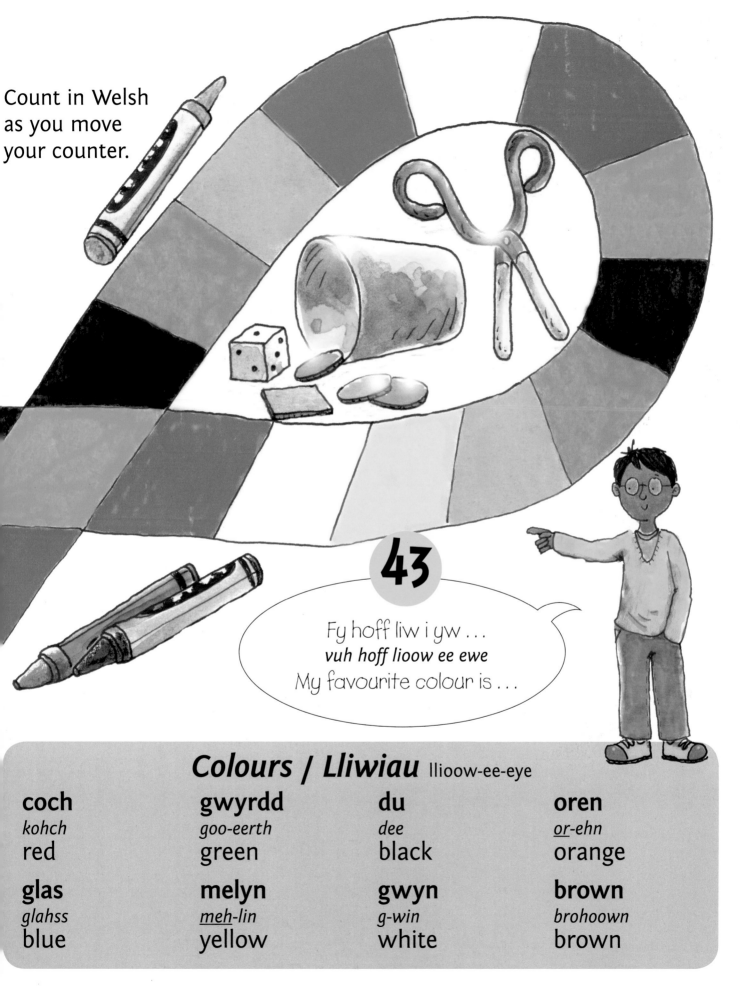

Count in Welsh as you move your counter.

43

Fy hoff liw i yw . . .
vuh hoff lioow ee ewe
My favourite colour is . . .

Colours / Lliwiau llioow-ee-eye

coch	**gwyrdd**	**du**	**oren**
kohch	*goo-eerth*	*dee*	*<u>or</u>-ehn*
red	green	black	orange
glas	**melyn**	**gwyn**	**brown**
glahss	*<u>meh</u>-lin*	*g-win*	*brohoown*
blue	yellow	white	brown

Ble wyt ti'n mynd?

These children are all dressed for their holidays. See if you can match the right phrases to the children. Say **Ble wyt ti'n mynd?** and then choose the right answering phrase. Practise saying this out loud too. Check your answers on page 32.

44

Ble wyt ti'n mynd?
bleh oiy-t teen mihnd?
Where are you going?

45

Dwi'n mynd i'r traeth
dween mihnd eer tr-eye-th
I'm going to the beach

46

Dwi'n mynd i'r wlad
dween mihnd eer ooow-lad
I'm going to the country

47

Dwi'n mynd i'r mynyddoedd
dween mihnd eer muhn-uhth-oith
I'm going to the mountains

48

Dwi'n mynd i'r dre
dween mihnd eer dray
I'm going to (the) town

Words to Know

ar wyliau
arr <u>wi</u>-lee-eye
on holiday

Siwrnai dda!
shoorn-eye <u>thah</u>
Have a good journey!

Dwi'n gwisgo . . .

It is time to get dressed – in Welsh! Have a look at the first picture and say **Dwi'n gwisgo trowsus bach**. Now look at the second picture and describe the difference in the trousers. Say **Dwi'n gwisgo trowsus mawr**. Carry on describing the differences between the clothes on page 31. You'll need to use the **Words to Know** and have a look at the note about how to say 'big' and 'small' in Welsh. You can check the answers on page 32.

Big or Small?

Sometimes in Welsh, the first letter of a word changes, depending on what has come before it. This is called a MUTATION (TREIGLAD). If the noun you are describing is feminine (marked below with an *****), **mawr** will become **fawr** and **bach** will become **fach**. Like this: **cot fawr** or **cot fach**; **sgert fawr** or **sgert fach**.

Words to Know

trowsus	**crys-T**	***sgert**	**bach / fach**
troh-oowsis	*crease tee*	*sghert*	*bahch / vahch*
trousers	T-shirt	skirt	small
*cot	**cap**	***siwmper**	**mawr / fawr**
cot	*cap*	*shoowmper*	*mahoor / vahoor*
coat	cap	jumper	big

Atebion / Answers

Here are the answers to the activities on pages 2–3, 14–15, 28–9 and 30–1

pages 2–3

4 Nos da

2 Hwyl fawr

1 Helô, bore da

3 Noswaith dda

pages 14–15

Dyma'r fam

Dyma'r tad-cu

Dyma'r ferch / chwaer

Dyma'r mab / brawd

pages 28–9

47 Dwi'n mynd i'r mynyddoedd

45 Dwi'n mynd i'r traeth

48 Dwi'n mynd i'r dre

46 Dwi'n mynd i'r wlad

pages 30–1

Dwi'n gwisgo cot fawr

Dwi'n gwisgo cot fach

Dwi'n gwisgo crys-T mawr

Dwi'n gwisgo crys-T bach

Dwi'n gwisgo siwmper fawr

Dwi'n gwisgo siwmper fach

Dwi'n gwisgo cap mawr

Dwi'n gwisgo cap bach

Brawddegau Cymraeg / Welsh Phrases

1 **Helô, bore da** Hello, good morning

2 **Hwyl fawr** Goodbye

3 **Noswaith dda** Good evening

4 **Nos da** Goodnight

5 **Beth yw dy enw di?** What's your name?

6 **Fy enw i yw . . .** My name is . . .

7 **A ti?** And you?

8 **Faint yw dy oed di?** How old are you?

9 **Dwi'n naw oed** I am nine years old

10 **Pen-blwydd hapus!** Happy birthday!

11 **Sut wyt ti?** How are you?

12 **Dwi'n iawn, diolch** I'm fine, thanks

13 **Dwi ddim yn dda** I'm not so well

14 **Ble mae'r . . .?** Where is . . .?

15 **Mae'r . . . fan hyn** Here is the . . .

16 **Tria eto!** Try again!

17 **Beth yw e / hi? / Beth ydy o / hi?** What is it?

18 **. . . yw e / hi / . . . ydy o / hi** It's a . . .

19 **Dyma'r mab** Here's the son

20 **Dyma'r ferch** Here's the daughter

21 **Dyma'r teulu** Here's the family

22 **Dwi'n hoffi . . .** I like . . .

23 **Dwi ddim yn hoffi . . .** I don't like . . .

24 **Ble wyt ti'n byw?** Where do you live?

25 **Dwi'n byw mewn tŷ** I live in a house

26 **Dwi'n byw mewn fflat** I live in an apartment

27 **Dwi'n byw yn y dre** I live in (the) town

28 **Dwi'n byw yn y wlad** I live in the country

29 **Ga i . . .** May I have . . .

30 **Os gwelwch yn dda** Please

31 **Dyna'r cwbwl, diolch** That's all, thanks

32 **Beth hoffet ti?** What would you like?

33 **Dwi'n llwglyd** I'm hungry

34 **Dwi'n sychedig** I'm thirsty

35 **Gwydraid o ddŵr** A glass of water

36 **Beth wyt ti eisiau wneud?** What do you want to do?

37 **Dwi eisiau gwylio'r teledu** I want to watch TV

38 **Dwi eisiau chwarae pêl-droed** I want to play football

39 **Dwi eisiau seiclo** I want to cycle

40 **Dwi eisiau mynd i nofio** I want to go swimming

41 **Pa liw yw e / Pa liw ydy o?** What colour is it?

42 **Beth yw dy hoff liw di?** What's your favourite colour?

43 **Fy hoff liw i yw . . .** My favourite colour is . . .

44 **Ble wyt ti'n mynd?** Where are you going?

45 **Dwi'n mynd i'r traeth** I'm going to the beach

46 **Dwi'n mynd i'r wlad** I'm going to the country

47 **Dwi'n mynd i'r mynyddoedd** I'm going to the mountains

48 **Dwi'n mynd i'r dre** I'm going to (the) town

49 **Dwi'n gwisgo trowsus bach** I'm wearing small trousers

50 **Dwi'n gwisgo trowsus mawr** I'm wearing big trousers